Parent Group Handbook for Calming the Family STORM

Gary D. McKay, Ph.D.

Impact Publishers®
ATASCADERO, CALIFORNIA

ATTENTION ORGANIZATIONS AND CORPORATIONS:
This book is available at quantity discounts on bulk purchases for educational, business, or sales promotional use. For further information, please contact Impact Publishers, P.O. Box 6016, Atascadero, CA 93423-6016, Phone: 1-800-246-7228. E-mail: sales@impactpublishers.com

Publisher's Note
This publication is designed to provide accurate and authoritative information in regard to the subject matter covered. It is sold with the understanding that the publisher is not engaged in rendering psychological, medical, or other professional services. If expert assistance or counseling is needed, the services of a competent professional should be sought.

Impact Publishers and colophon are registered trademarks of Impact Publishers, Inc.

Cover design by K.A. White, San Luis Obispo, California

Interior design by Sue Knopf/Graffolio, La Crosse, Wisconsin

Printed in the United States of America on acid-free paper.

Published by **Impact Publishers®**
POST OFFICE BOX 6016
ATASCADERO, CALIFORNIA 93423-6016
www.impactpublishers.com

Contents

Introduction

This parent group handbook for *Calming the Family Storm* is based on my experience as a coauthor with the late Don Dinkmeyer and others in developing the *Systematic Training for Effective Parenting (STEP)* programs, other group programs, and working with parent and anger management study groups over the years. Through this experience, I have learned the value of study groups. While many people can learn human relationship concepts from simply reading a book, study groups can help people learn to apply the concepts through dialogue with others and the group leader.

The purpose of this book study group is to help participants:

♦ Improve their family relationships by learning to apply the principles of anger management presented by the authors.

♦ Receive feedback on their challenges with their families.

♦ Learn from the experience of others.

There's a lot of material to cover in each session, so organization is of vital importance. In Part 2: "Scheduling Group Meetings — How Many and How Often?" I will discuss different ways to divide up the book into manageable pieces for adequate group discussion.

The guide is divided into the following parts:

Part 1: Finding Group Members — They're All Around You

Part 2: Scheduling Group Meetings — How Many and How Often?

Part 3: Organizing Your Group — What to Do When You Get Them Together

Part 4: Leading Your Group — Tips for Keeping Them on Track

Part 5: Session Format — How to Organize Each Session

Part 6: Study Guide for *Calming the Family Storm* — Chapter by Chapter

I hope your experience working with parenting groups is as satisfying as mine.

— Gary D. McKay, Ph.D.

PART 1

Finding Group Members —
They're All Around You

Since *Calming the Family Storm* is about managing family anger. and even though there is information about couples in the book, most, if not all, of the people interested in your group will be parents. Some will be married, others divorced and single parents, some in non-married couple relationships, and some in stepfamilies. So, since most will be parents, where do you find parents? Schools, religious groups, counseling agencies, family or juvenile court, children's recreation programs, Child Protective Services (CPS), and other community organizations all involve parents.

FINDING PARENTS

If you've organized parenting groups, you probably know how to generate participants. If you're new at this, the following suggestions should help. The more of these ideas you use, the greater chance you have of generating a group.

In the following section — "Publicizing the Class" — you'll find a sample flyer and advertising poster for announcing your study group. (You may want to scan these into your computer, or copy, cut and paste and duplicate.)

Schools may send notices home with kids or have a newsletter. Perhaps you can give a talk at a PTA or PTO meeting. You can introduce the concept of family anger management and publicize the group.

Religious organizations may be willing to include a flyer or notice in their bulletins or pass out flyers after a worship service. Some may let you make a verbal announcement during the service as well.

Sending flyers to local counseling agencies or therapists in private practice in your community can also help generate participants. If you belong to a local professional organization(s) you may be permitted to publicize with their website or newsletter.

Anger management is of interest to the legal system. Get in touch with court officials in family or juvenile court and social workers in CPS and let them know the service you will be providing. Courts and CPS in most communities have a list of services they give to mandated parents. You'll need to find out what the requirements for mandated parents are in terms of time spent in class, as well as what forms or certificates you have to sign for these group members. Also, your community may have family mediation services and/or attorneys who offer collaborative law services. Those professionals may be interested in suggesting that parents attend your study group.

A Word About Working with Courts*

In order to be on a court's referral list for mandated people, you must be approved by the court. If you work for an agency that is on the referral list, then you can receive court referrals through your agency.

If you're in private practice and want to work directly with the courts, then call each court and see what they require. Realize that getting approval on your own is a challenging task — often an uphill struggle. So your best bet may be to affiliate with a court approved agency for this service and work under their umbrella, receiving referrals the courts make to the agency.

Of course you have to have the right credentials. Perhaps you're certified or licensed as a counselor, marriage and family therapist, social worker or psychologist and can provide information on your experience in working with families and/or parents. The agency or court may want to see the curriculum you intend to use. You can show them a copy of *Calming the Family Storm* and this parent leader's guide.

* Many thanks to Barbara Mountjoy, a Pennsylvania attorney; Ken Wong, Teen Program Director for Redmond, Washington; and Kent Baker, a therapist in Tucson, Arizona, for their assistance with this information about the courts.

Publicizing the Class

Local TV stations may be interested in publicizing your group. Perhaps you can get an interview during a news program. Contact the producers at the news departments, or the news announcers. Contact information is usually provided by local stations' websites or the phone book.

You can also post flyers or notices on organizations' **websites** visited by professionals who work with families. Another idea is to get on your professional organization's Listserve so that you can send emails to other professionals announcing your study group.

Some study group leaders like to use **online chat groups** for discussion. If this is of interest to you, you could possibly run a chat group through a professional organization's website. Or perhaps your agency or you have a website and you can set it up that way. You'll need to purchase copies of the book to send out to chat group members, or ask them to check their local book stores, or order copies online.

You can design a **flyer** announcing your group which can be sent to your various contacts or posted on websites. On the next page is an example. (You could also copy this one and fill in your own information.)

Some leaders like to make a large **poster** which can be displayed in school faculty lounges, agencies, churches, grocery stores, etc. The poster would simply announce the class and give contact information (see sample at right).

Most **newspapers** and some websites want a brief announcement. You could use the same format suggested for the poster to design these announcements. Most local newspapers give free space for announcements of community activities. You could design a notice for your study group. You may also be able to get an interview. Some public places parents frequent, such as grocery stores, will also let you post a notice on their bulletin board.

When people register, you'll want to get in touch before the first meeting. In Part 3: "Organizing Your Group — What to Do When You Get Them Together," you'll find a sample letter you can send to participants giving the dates and chapters which will be discussed in each session, followed by suggestions for making the discussion a worthwhile experience.

When people contact you, you can give them the details of the class such as cost, and how to get books. You could also send them a signup form and the letter with the chapter assignments and suggestions for making the discussion a worthwhile experience (See Part 3). If they have email, you could send this information as an email attachment.

Part 2: "Scheduling Group Meetings — How Many and How Often?" will give you ideas on time limits, frequency of meetings, number of sessions, size of group, and member commitment.

Family Anger Management Class

Featuring the book:

Calming the Family Storm
Anger Management for Moms, Dads and All the Kids

Authors:
Gary D. McKay, Ph.D.
and Steven A. Maybell, Ph.D.

Class conducted by:
(Name, degree, agency/school)

Time and Dates:

Place:

Contact:

Family Anger Management Class

Featuring the book:

Calming the Family Storm

Anger Management for Moms, Dads and All the Kids

Authors: Gary D. McKay, Ph.D. and Steven A. Maybell, Ph.D.

Class conducted by: *(Name, degree, agency/school)*

In the class you will learn:

- How anger develops, why we get angry, and the purposes anger serves in our lives.
- Strategies to get anger under control quickly.
- Ways to change your life so you don't get angry so much.
- How to develop encouraging relationships in your family.
- How to get along better even when you're angry.
- Techniques for problem solving and family meetings.
- How to discipline without anger.
- A proven approach to couples' intimate communication, including anger.
- How to teach children how to handle their anger with each other and with adults.
- Anger issues related to divorce, single parenting, and stepfamilies.
- About the all-too-common problem of domestic violence.

Time and Dates:

Place:

Fee: (A copy of the book is included in the fee.)*

Contact: *(You could also include a signup form in the flyer)*

---

* NOTE: If you've decided to have members purchase books at a local book store or online, you would give this information here, including the cost of the book, and your fee would be in addition to the cost of the book.

PART 2

Scheduling Group Meetings —
How Many and How Often?

In this part I discuss time limits and frequency, group size and member commitment. The suggestions are based on my experience. You may have some different ideas.

TIME LIMITS AND FREQUENCY

TIME LIMITS

I've found a one-and-a-half- or two-hour session per week is the best organization for most study groups. Shorter time periods create a rush through the material and longer periods may create boredom or fatigue. Once a week seems to be the best frequency as it gives time for participants to experiment with the ideas.

There are exceptions to the above guidelines. If your situation calls for more frequent, shorter meetings, or fewer long ones, you will need to adjust the following suggested schedules. If you choose to meet longer than two hours, I recommend that a short break be taken during the session.

NUMBER OF SESSIONS

Following are three suggested session plans — a six-week plan, a seven-week plan for one and a half- or two-hour sessions which could be taught, for example, in the evenings, and a four-session weekend plan which might be taught on four consecutive Saturday mornings with two and one-half or three-hour sessions including a break. You can photocopy the organization of your choice, fill in the date column and duplicate as a handout for your group members so they know what the chapter assignments are for each session and how to prepare for a session.

Six-Session Plan

SESSION	DATE	CHAPTERS DISCUSSED
1		Chapter 1: "One Big Happy Family....or Is It?"
		Chapter 2: "The Anatomy of Anger"
		Chapter 3: "Anger Management Strategies I — First Steps"
		Chapter 4: "Anger Management Strategies II — For the Long Term"
		Chapter 5: "Five Steps to Less Anger in Your Life"
2		Chapter 6: "Encouraging Relationships"
		Chapter 7: "Healthy Communication
3		Chapter 8: "Problem Solving and Conflict Resolution"
		Chapter 9: "Family and Couple Meetings"
		Chapter 10: "All's Fair in Love..."
4		Chapter 11: "Discipline Without Anger"
		Chapter 12: "Children's Choices and Consequences"
5		Chapter 13: "When Kids Get Angry"
		Chapter 14: "Anger Management for Kids"
6		Chapter 15: "Angry Divorces, Single Parents, Stepfamilies"
		Chapter 16: "When Anger Turns to Violence"
		Chapter 17: "Beyond the Family Storm"

SEVEN-SESSION PLAN

SESSION	DATE	CHAPTERS DISCUSSED
1		Chapter 1: "One Big Happy Family....or Is It?"
		Chapter 2: "The Anatomy of Anger"
		Chapter 3: "Anger Management Strategies I — First Steps"
2		Chapter 4: "Anger Management Strategies II — For the Long Term"
		Chapter 5: "Five Steps to Less Anger in Your Life"
3		Chapter 6: "Encouraging Relationships"
		Chapter 7: "Healthy Communication
4		Chapter 8: "Problem Solving and Conflict Resolution"
		Chapter 9: "Family and Couple Meetings"
		Chapter 10: "All's Fair in Love..."
5		Chapter 11: "Discipline Without Anger"
		Chapter 12: "Children's Choices and Consequences"
6		Chapter 13: "When Kids Get Angry"
		Chapter 14: "Anger Management for Kids"
7		Chapter 15: "Angry Divorces, Single Parents, Stepfamilies"
		Chapter 16: "When Anger Turns to Violence"
		Chapter 17: "Beyond the Family Storm"

FOUR-SESSION WEEKEND PLAN

SESSION	DATE	CHAPTERS DISCUSSED
1		Chapter 1: "One Big Happy Family....or Is It?"
		Chapter 2: "The Anatomy of Anger"
		Chapter 3: "Anger Management Strategies I — First Steps"
		Chapter 4: "Anger Management Strategies II — For the Long Term"
		Chapter 5: "Five Steps to Less Anger in Your Life"
2		Chapter 6: "Encouraging Relationships"
		Chapter 7: "Healthy Communication
		Chapter 8: "Problem Solving and Conflict Resolution"
		Chapter 9: "Family and Couple Meetings"
3		Chapter 10: "All's Fair in Love..."
		Chapter 11: "Discipline Without Anger"
		Chapter 12: "Children's Choices and Consequences"
		Chapter 13: "When Kids Get Angry"
		Chapter 14: "Anger Management for Kids"
4		Chapter 15: "Angry Divorces, Single Parents, Stepfamilies"
		Chapter 16: "When Anger Turns to Violence"
		Chapter 17: "Beyond the Family Storm"

GROUP SIZE

Benefits for members of a study group are best when there's opportunity for each member to:

- ◆ Ask questions about the concepts and skills presented in the book.
- ◆ Participate in the discussion and any exercises used during a session.
- ◆ Discuss application of the concepts and skills to his or her family.

Given these guidelines, experience shows that ten to twelve members is the maximum for an effective study group experience. If more people are interested in attending the group than the maximum, you have several choices:

1. Establish a second group at another time.
2. Refer excess members to another experience.
3. Develop a waiting list.
4. Include the extra members in your group and divide the group into small groups to discuss questions and do any exercises you assign. At the conclusion of the small group experiences, let each group report the results of its discussion to the entire group so that all may benefit.

MEMBER COMMITMENT

This study group is not designed to be a "drop-in" experience as the topics are sequential. It's important that group members realize they are committing to attend each session of the group. Of course there will be legitimate reasons that a member can't attend a session such as family illness, emergency or prior commitment.

You may have mandated group members who will require a signature on a form or certificate showing they've attended the class. If these people miss sessions you will have to determine whether or not they are absent for legitimate reasons and whether you have met the requirements of the mandate.

Members should understand that they are expected to read the assigned material to prepare for discussion. Other assignments involve journaling and experimenting with the ideas and skills (Action Steps). Just reading and discussing the book won't "calm the family storm." Application is essential.

Part 3, discusses how to organize your group — what to do when you get them together, including describing the purpose of the class and introductions, assessing the goals of each member, and setting the ground rules for group discussion.

Organizing Your Group —
What to Do When You Get Them Together

In this part we'll discuss how you can prepare for your first session, conduct an optional orientation session, use an "ice breaker" exercise, and discuss members' goals and ground rules for discussion.

PREPARING FOR THE FIRST SESSION

BOOK DISTRIBUTION

It's best to distribute books before the first session. This allows you to give the reading assignment for the first session so that the members are prepared for the discussion. You can have members drop by your office or agency to pick up their books, or mail copies to them, or you can arrange with a local bookstore to have the books on hand for the members to purchase. Suggesting that members purchase the books online through companies like Amazon.com or directly from Impactpublishers.com is another option.

SAMPLE LETTER TO ENROLLEES

You can send a letter to enrollees giving the dates and chapters which will be discussed in each session, followed by suggestions for making the discussion a worthwhile experience. (Or, if you've designed a publicity flyer, you could include this information in the flyer, eliminating the need to send it separately.)

The sample letter on the next page shows the information you'll want to include in your correspondence with your group members. If you have them purchase the book at a local bookstore or online, send the information to them in a letter, fax, or email.

NAME PLACARDS

To help you and the group remember names of participants and their family members, it helps to have name and family information placards.

To: *[name or just Group Member]*

Re: Family Anger Management Class with *Calming the Family Storm: Anger Management for Moms, Dads and All the Kids*

Dear Group Member:

In each session, we will discuss chapters of the book. Below are the dates and chapters which will be discussed in each session. Also, suggestions are included for making the discussion a worthwhile experience for you.

If you have any questions, please call _____

[Insert dates of the class and chapter assignments here. See Part 2: "Scheduling Group Meetings — How Many and How Often?" for possible schedules which could be copied and included in your letter, and continue with the following suggestions.]

SUGGESTIONS FOR MAKING THE DISCUSSION A WORTHWHILE EXPERIENCE

1. Come prepared. There's a lot to read between sessions, including preparing for our first session. You may want to read the assigned chapters for each session all in one sitting or spread them out over several days between sessions — whatever works for you.

2. Use the ideas in the book with your family. Don't just try to put an idea into practice, actually do it. Trying and doing aren't the same thing. Make a commitment to use an idea for a specific period of time — between sessions (unless something dangerous happens, of course — which is rare), then evaluate your progress. Don't overdo it by attempting to use all the ideas in the book at once. Manageable "chunks" — ideas from the book called "Action Steps" — will be assigned at the end of each session.

3. Bring your questions, comments and reports on your experiences with the ideas for discussion. Write in the margins or start a journal (in chapter 3 of the book journaling is introduced).

4. You can use the following questions as guidelines for your study of the chapters. We will discuss these questions in each class meeting.
   - What did you learn from the reading?
   - Which ideas in the reading were particularly helpful? Why?
   - How would you apply the ideas in the chapters to your family?
   - Are there any questions about the reading?

Use an 8½ by 11 sheet of card stock, folded lengthwise so that it will "stand" on the table — or floor if members aren't seated around a table — in front of them. Note: you can also cut file folders in half lengthwise and fold each side in half.

In the first session, ask each member to put the following information on his or her placard:

- Name
- Name of spouse/partner and/or ex beneath his or her name.
- Names and ages of their children in descending order — oldest to the youngest.

So, the information would look something like this:

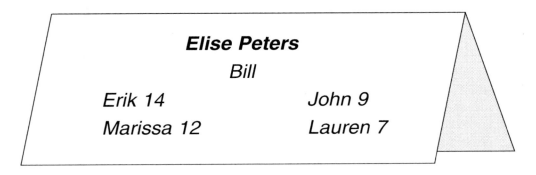

If Elise is a single parent and Bill is her ex, Bill's name would be in parentheses. If she was married before, and Bill is her current husband, she would put the name of her ex in parentheses under Bill's name. If some of the kids are her stepchildren, she would put an * (asterisk) before the names. These markings help you identify what might be the dynamics of the family.

OPTIONAL ORIENTATION SESSION

Some leaders prefer to add an orientation session, in which the members get acquainted, receive copies of the book and reading assignments, discuss their expectations or goals for the group, and go over ground rules. (See page 17.) You may also have a favorite "ice breaker" or warm-up exercise you'd like to use. There's an exercise on the next page by my co-author, Dr. Steven A. Maybell, which can be used.

Others prefer to tack the orientation onto the first session, so they distribute the books, review the Major Points for the chapters covered in the first session and have members read and discuss parts of the book during that first class.

For those who prefer not to use an orientation session, goals or expectations and ground rules can also be part of the first session, as stated in the session guides. Some leaders like to add about 15 minutes to the first session to go over the goals and ground rules, so that the full one-and-a-half- or two-hour time slot can be devoted to discussion and application of the material in the assigned chapters.

"ICE BREAKER" WARM-UP EXERCISE

What's Up With Anger?

Purpose

1. More connection.
2. Help group participants begin to think about anger in a more holistic way.
3. Plant some seeds about the purpose and benefits of the course.

Directions

Have the participants answer the following questions. This may be done in small groups of three or four or with the class as a whole. If you use small groups have one member of each group act as note-taker and jot down the responses from the group. When the small groups have finished, each group's note-taker reports their group's discussion to the full class, and the leader jots down each response on a board (or butcher paper). If the exercise is done with the whole group, write down all of the responses on the board (or butcher paper).

You can write these questions on a board (or butcher paper):

1. What is anger?
2. What causes anger?
3. What impact does anger have on the angry person; on relationships?
4. How can we better manage anger within ourselves; in our relationships?

After all the responses have been provided and clarified, you can say something like: *"There are clearly many ideas people have about anger. It can be a confusing and complicated topic. In this class, the important things you will learn about include:*

1. *Every human being experiences anger; it is a common human emotion.*
2. *Anger has both advantages and disadvantages.*
3. *Anger, if not managed effectively, can cause great harm in our families.*
4. *There is more to understanding anger than most people realize.*
5. *Every human being can get better at managing anger and responding to the anger of others.*

This class will contribute to everyone's understanding of the common myths about anger, what leads to anger, how we can better manage our own anger and help our family members with their anger, respond more effectively to family storms, small and large, and understand and deal with children's misbehavior in effective, non-angry ways."

MEMBERS' GOALS FOR THE CLASS AND DISCUSSION GROUND RULES

I suggest the following information be given in your orientation session — should you decide to have a separate orientation session — or, in your first session.

PURPOSE OF THE CLASS AND INTRODUCTIONS

Introduce yourself and state the purpose of the class. You could say something like: "The purpose of this class is to study and discuss the book *Calming the Family Storm: Anger Management for Moms, Dads, and All the Kids* and to apply the book's concepts to your families."

Ask members to fill out the name placards described above.

ASSESSING THE GOALS OF EACH MEMBER

Assessing goals lets you know what the group expects, helps them see that in many ways they are similar, and lets you clear up any misconceptions of the purpose of the group, should there be any.

Ask each member to answer this question: "What do you want to learn from this experience?" Look for similarities and link and summarize. (See "Group Leadership Skills" in Part 3).

You could follow up with asking each group member to complete the sentence, "I get angry when . . . " The information gained from this exercise helps you and the members see the types of anger issues faced by the group.

DISCUSSING GROUND RULES FOR GROUP DISCUSSION

Tell the group that in order for everyone to have a beneficial group experience, certain guidelines or ground rules must be followed. You could print these rules as a handout or put them on a poster and display it during each session where everyone can see it, or both. The following seven ground rules will help you conduct a productive group. Explain each rule and its purpose to the group. As the group proceeds, if you find members violating the rules, you could say something like: "What ground rule are we forgetting?"

1. Stick to the topic
This rule will help keep the group focused on the task. There may be times when a member will change the subject before the group has adequately dealt with it. Or a member will go off on a tangent. In either case, you will call the group's attention to this and suggest they return to the topic under discussion.

2. Take part in the discussion
The group benefits the most when everyone is involved. Encourage group members to comment when they have an idea based on what they're learning that they think will be helpful or a question about the topic under discussion. If members are frequently silent, you may ask them if they have any thoughts to share.

3. Give everyone a chance to participate
The purpose of the group is for all members to have the opportunity to discuss what they are learning. Sometimes group members will monopolize discussions. If this happens, you may intervene and ask other members for their ideas, questions or concerns.

4. Have patience — change takes time
Instant change, though possible, is rare. Remind the group that change takes time but the effort is well worth it. Encourage members to make a commitment to use a procedure for a specified length of time, such as a week (between sessions) and then evaluate the results.

5.   Encourage your fellow group members

As members will learn in Chapter 6, "Encouraging Relationships," encouragement is vital to anger management and healthy relationships. Group members will benefit from being encouraged in the group. The encouragement of the group aids in stimulating change and helps members learn by example how to encourage their families and themselves. Ask the group to observe and comment on each other's strengths, progress and efforts.

6.   Take responsibility for your choices

Remind the group that the only person one can change is oneself. Taking responsibility for and changing one's beliefs, purposes and behavior will have an influence on their family members. Encourage them to take responsibility in the group as well by making sure their comments are helpful.

7.   Maintain confidentiality

What's said in the group stays in the group. (This is especially important when you have members in the group who are court mandated.) Members are free to talk outside the group about the concepts and skills they are learning and sharing their own personal issues, but not the issues of others in the group. (Of course this rule doesn't apply to you if you suspect child abuse.)

NOTE: If you work for an agency, your organization may have certain policies and procedures or forms to have group participants complete — for example, a form for group members to sign agreeing to maintain as confidential information shared in the group by other group members. There also may be municipal, state or federal laws for you to discuss and implement in this first group session. For example, disclosing that you are a mandated reporter of abuse, having clients sign a form verifying that you have reviewed confidentiality rules, mandatory reporting responsibilities and your professional credentials.

Part 4: "Leading Your Group — Tips for Keeping Them on Track" will give you information about your role as a leader, skills for effective group leadership, how to deal with resistance, and a word about mandated participants.

PART 4

Leading Your Group —
Tips for Keeping Them On Track

Leadership is challenging and requires certain personal qualities, effort, commitment and skills. In this part of the manual, you'll learn what it takes to be an effective group leader, leadership role and skills, what to do about resistance and how to work with mandated group members.

WHAT DOES IT TAKE TO BE AN EFFECTIVE GROUP LEADER?

Effective group leaders have certain personal qualities. While they may judge behavior as helpful or not helpful to a person and/or his or her family, they don't judge the person. They "separate the deed from the doer," realizing that all people are fallible yet worthwhile as human beings.

These leaders are people who are sensitive to the concerns and feelings of the group members. They listen, they care, and they show their understanding of feelings, beliefs and behaviors. Their tone of voice, body language and choice of words are encouraging. They put the group's needs above their own and demonstrate mutual respect.

Such people are constantly on the lookout for positive group behaviors and comment on such behaviors. For example, when the group encourages a member, they may ask how that member feels and point out the importance of encouragement to the group.

Effective leaders believe in people's ability to make positive changes. They notice even small movement toward better family relationships and ask the group for feedback or give feedback to the person themselves. Such leaders persevere; they don't give up on people, avoiding the thought, "He (she) will never change." They recognize that resistance to change indicates discouragement, and are quick to find ways to encourage the person, hearing his or her discouragement, pointing out effort and improvement. They are enthusiastic about possibilities — they encourage their group members to use the ideas they are learning, not expecting perfection. Such leaders "have the courage to be imperfect," and their acceptance of mistakes group members may make helps members develop that courage as well. At the same time, they are patient, realizing how tough change can be.

Given these personal qualities, let's take a closer look at the role of an effective leader, followed by leadership skills to help you implement your role.

LEADERSHIP ROLE

Your job as a leader is to engage the group in discussion and application of the concepts and skills presented in *Calming the Family Storm*. Even if you're an expert in anger management and/or family education, it's best if you don't come across as such. It's important to get everyone's questions and ideas concerning the material. They are peers and mostly "all in the same boat." They can be valuable resources for helping each other.

This is not to say that you should not give an opinion. Your opinion counts too. But if you attempt to answer every question and continually give advice, you may be putting yourself on a pedestal and therefore vulnerable to being knocked off. So keep your ego in check and give your opinion only when it's needed and after group members have had an opportunity to comment. (Remember, you're not Dr. Phil!)

Basically, your role is to organize the group, facilitate discussion and keep the group on track. Your ability to listen well and facilitate communication among group members will be a great benefit to the group.

If a question comes up and is directed to you, you can redirect it to the group: "What do you think about that?"; "What do the authors say about that?"; "How would you have handled the situation?" By doing so you'll tap the wisdom of the group and "universalize" the problem posed by the question.

Redirecting a question stimulates, involves, and brings the group together. It also shows your belief in peoples' ability to understand and apply the concepts.

GROUP LEADERSHIP SKILLS

The leadership skills discussed below are similar to the ones in chapter 9, "Family and Couple Meetings," in *Calming the Family Storm*. They are expanded a bit and adapted to a study group as opposed to a couple or family meeting. By using these skills, you not only help the group function constructively, you serve as a model for them for conducting effective family and couple meetings.

Structuring sets the tone and purpose of the group — to study, discuss and apply the concepts and skills in the book to specific family situations and to encourage each other. Sometimes group members may wander off task. If this happens, you can structure by asking a simple question: "How does this relate to the topic?"

The leader who structures well senses when it's appropriate to allow leeway in discussion and when it's best to move on with the topic at hand, or move to a new topic.

Universalizing is the process of helping group members become aware that their questions and concerns are often shared by others. So, when someone poses a question or is concerned about an issue, you can simply ask, "Has anyone else wondered about (or experienced) that?" or, "Has anyone had problems in applying . . . ?" As group members respond, others may realize they are not alone. It's especially important to universalize in early meetings as people begin to realize that their concerns are pretty common and that they don't need to be afraid to share.

Linking is the identification of common and unique or different themes in two or more members' comments. This skill aids in universalizing.

Suppose Katie complains about her son's refusal to do his homework — and an angry exchange occurs between the mom and her child. Armando gets angry when his daughter won't go to bed on time. The situations are different in behavior, but the goal is the same — each child wants power. Linking these two problems and helping the group realize the similarity — a power contest — helps the members learn to apply the concepts and skills they are learning. Each parent needs to learn how to back out of the power contest, get control of his or her own anger and find ways the child can use the desire for power constructively.

On the other hand, on the surface some problems may seem the same, yet are actually different. Chen's son is failing math and Chen is in a constant battle with him regarding this issue. Kellie's child is also failing math, but she has given up, believing her daughter just can't do it. So we have the same behavior — failing math — but the kids have different goals: Chen's child is seeking power and Kellie's child is displaying inadequacy. Each situation requires a different parental response.

You can establish a link by asking the group questions such as "These behaviors are different, but there seems to be some similarity as well. How are these two situations similar?" Or, "On the surface these two behaviors seem similar, both kids are . . ., but what is unique about each situation?"

Redirecting involves maximizing involvement by inviting participation from all members. It's important that members learn to talk with each other and not just with the leader. So, when comments and questions are posed to you, you can redirect by asking members what they think, and then add your opinion if necessary.

Redirecting also helps involve silent members. "Ken, we haven't heard from you on this, is there something you'd like to say about it?" Of course a member can decline comment, but at least you have given him or her an opportunity to speak about the issue.

Another aspect of redirecting involves "brainstorming." Brainstorming is the process of getting everyone's ideas before making a decision. The process is useful when a participant is asking for help in solving a problem with his or her family member. You explain the process and then ask for suggestions. "Let's brainstorm some ideas for Maria. In brainstorming we give all the ideas we can think of and hold off evaluation until we're finished. This way we encourage creative thinking. If ideas are rejected as they're given, we may discourage other members from giving their ideas for fear they will be unacceptable. Maria, are you willing to listen to all the ideas we generate — even if you don't like some of them — and withhold comment until we're finished? Is everyone else willing to withhold judgment too?"

When finished with the brainstorming, you can ask which idea or ideas appeal to the group member. Ask the member why he or she chose a particular idea. This gives you information on whether or not the member really understands the dynamics of the situation. If the member chooses an idea you think will be a problem in the relationship, you can ask the group, "What might happen if Maria does that?" The final decision is up to Maria, of course, but she has feedback from the group to take into consideration.

If the member indicates none of the suggestions are helpful, the group can brainstorm again or table the issue (if it's not an emergency) until the next session, when people may come up with other ideas. However, if you think one or more of the ideas would be helpful, give your opinion. If the person still rejects the ideas, his or her level of understanding may be the issue, or the member is resisting and has no desire to change, or is too discouraged to do so. You and the group can address these issues. Again, realize that the decision is up to the member.

Promoting direct interaction means getting members to talk to each other rather than going through the leader. Members often talk to each other through the leader — it's as if they are speaking different languages and you are the translator. A member may say something like "I think he should . . . ." You can promote direct interaction by saying, "Please tell . . . directly." If you do this enough times, the group members will catch on.

Promoting direct interaction stimulates group involvement and helps keep you out of the expert role. It also helps build group cohesiveness.

Giving feedback is a skill which helps group members learn how they are perceived by others in the group. This knowledge can help them discover how they may be coming across to their family members. The receiver of the feedback decides whether or not to act on the information.

Appropriate ways to give feedback can be encouraged by modeling. "When you told me how you talked to (your partner, child, or ex) I found myself feeling threatened. I wonder if your (family member) might feel that way too." You can also ask the group for feedback. "How does what Tony is saying come across to you?"

Talk about the purpose of feedback. That is, learning how we are perceived by others may give us insight as to how we are perceived by our family members.

Feedback is not limited to problems. It can also be given to encourage group members. "You really worked hard on the relationship this week. I'll bet you feel good about your accomplishment." Or, to the group: "How do you think Kristin is feeling about this?"

Feedback can also be used to help group members sort out their feelings through using reflective listening: "You feel hurt by Chuck's behavior because it seems like he doesn't respect you." Or you can ask the group how they think the member is feeling.

A word of caution: Some members may misunderstand the feedback process and make remarks which could be discouraging, such as "No wonder you're having problems with Jennifer. It seems like you're always talking down to her." If something like this happens, inform the member that his or her comment may be discouraging and ask if the member would be willing to rephrase the comment with an I-message.

For feedback to be accepted, the group must be cohesive and contain an atmosphere of mutual respect. For that reason, it's best to not give or ask for feedback in the first few sessions.

Exploring beliefs and purposes that create anger or relate to a child's goal of misbehavior can help improve relationships. In the book we discuss the beliefs which create anger, or the MADS: M – <u>M</u>inimizing personal power; A – <u>A</u>wfulizing; D – <u>D</u>emanding; S – <u>S</u>haming and blaming — the "hot thoughts." We also discuss the purposes of anger: control, winning, getting even or protecting rights.

When a member brings up an angry incident, explore his or her self-talk — the belief about what occurred. How is the member minimizing, awfulizing, demanding, and shaming and blaming? Then explore the purpose—what is the member trying to achieve by the anger — to control, win, get even, or protect rights? Ask the group to respectfully share what they observe.

Next, discuss with the member how he or she can create "cool thoughts" and positive purposes. Ask the group for suggestions. The group may need to consult the book to review methods for creating cool thoughts and positive purposes.

When discussing the misbehavior of a child, examine the four goals: attention, power, revenge, displaying inadequacy. Depending upon which session you're in, the group may have to look ahead or back for information on the four goals of misbehavior. Chart 1, "The Four Goals of Children's Misbehavior," in chapter 11 (page 170) gives a good overview of the goals and how to discover, by his or her misbehavior, which goal a child is seeking.

Giving encouragement involves accepting, instilling faith and confidence, accentuating the positive, building on strengths and promoting responsibility. Group members need as much encouragement as their family members.

Encouragement is vital to the success or failure of the group. When group members feel accepted and valued, they are more willing to attend sessions, participate and make changes.

Look for examples of effort as well as accomplishment. "You're really working hard on . . ." "You're learning to manage your anger more effectively." Ask the group what they notice. "What do you notice about the way Wayne is handling this situation now as opposed to a couple of weeks ago?"

Focus on how group members can apply encouragement in their families: "What are some ways Lynn can encourage Richard?"; "James, you seem to be able to see the big picture; how can you use this skill in your relationship with Vicki?"

Members will make mistakes; this is natural especially when one is attempting to make a change. Emphasize that the value of a mistake is learning what not to do. Mistakes can point one in a more appropriate direction. You can model acceptance and learning from mistakes by sharing your own examples. You can help a discouraged member develop faith in him- or herself by asking the group to point out the strengths they see in the member.

Setting tasks moves the group beyond the discussion of ideas in the book into action. Once you and the group have helped a member identify the dynamics of the problem, such as his or her beliefs and purposes, or what the "opponent" may be feeling and perceiving, and/or a child's goal of misbehavior, proceed with a decision on what to do about it and a *commitment* to follow through. "What are you willing to do this week to address this challenge?"; "How will you apply these ideas?" (Perhaps the member will want suggestions and the group can brainstorm.)

The commitment is not forever, just until the next session at which time the group member has an opportunity to discuss the results of the new procedure. At that point she or he can decide, based on the results, to continue the action, modify it or choose to do something else if need be.

The commitment is like doing an experiment; you use the procedure each time a given situation arises and judge the results after several trials (unless the results are dangerous, of course). Changes in another's behavior often don't occur after one or two incidents of a new action. After all, the problem has probably been going on for some time and there's been a payoff from the complaining member for the "opponent's" behavior. The "opponent" won't give it up until he or she finds it just won't work anymore.

Watch out for the "I'll try" game. Trying and doing aren't the same thing. If a person wants to change, then she or he must make the change, not just "try" to do it. Trying is like buying insurance against failure. When you try it and it doesn't work, you can say, "Well, at least I tried."

So, if a group member tells the group he or she will try, make a respectful confrontation: "When you say 'I'll try,' I get the feeling that you really don't want to do this, or that you don't believe it will work. Are you willing to experiment with this procedure until next session, despite the results (unless danger is involved) and we can review it then?" If the group member is still tentative about it, assure him or her that it's his or her decision. If the member decides not to do the task, would she or he be willing to just think about it? Most will commit to that. You may discover at the next session that the person thought about it and actually decided to do it!

Summarizing involves pulling together the discussion at any given point where a summary may be called for. At the end of a session is a good time for a summary, but there can be other times as well. Suppose there's a long discussion. Before moving to the next topic, you may want to summarize or call for a summary to see if the members understand the ideas just discussed. If there's disagreement, summarize before moving on: "It seems some of us think . . . and others of us think . . . , let's move on and we can revisit this later if need be."

These leadership skills will help you manage the group effectively. But what if you encounter resistance—what do you do then? The next section deals with types of resistance and how you can address each challenge.

DEALING WITH PROBLEM GROUP MEMBERS

When some people feel unsure of themselves they may get defensive and resist ideas. Consider the purpose of the resistance. Group members may resist because they fail to understand the concepts and skills, they have a different experience than the other group members or the situations in the book, they are skeptical of the effectiveness of a particular idea, or resistance is a pattern of their interaction with others.

Resistance means someone is at cross purposes with you, the group, or the ideas in the book. Your challenge is goal alignment between the resister and the group or the book's ideas. For example, both the resister and the other group members agree that gaining cooperation from family members is a legitimate objective. The problem is agreeing on what procedures are effective in achieving this goal — demanding cooperation through the use of anger, or winning cooperation through methods which demonstrate mutual respect?

What happens if you can't align goals between the resister and the group? Acknowledge that everyone has a right to his or her opinion and to accept or reject the book's concepts. Then move on.

The ground rules for group discussion listed in Part 3, "Organizing Your Group — What to Do When You Get Them Together," can often be used as reminders of the purpose of the group. Ask the group: "What discussion ground rule applies here?" In this way the group learns to manage itself. Suppose group members are getting into a power struggle; they are not taking responsibility for their own behavior — they are trying to make the other person see things as they do. So the rule that applies is "Take responsibility for your choices."

When someone challenges you or the book, you can redirect the discussion by simply asking others what they think. You can then structure the discussion by reminding the members of the purpose of the group — to study and learn how to apply the concepts of the book, emphasizing again that everyone is free to accept or reject an idea. Be sure to use the encouragement leadership skill by pointing out behavior and attitudes that are positive as well as hearing any discouragement.

RESISTANCE STYLES

There are several ways people can resist. Below is a discussion of the most common forms of resistance.

Challenging. Some group members resist by challenging you, other members, or ideas from the book. This can be quite disconcerting as it often stimulates defensiveness and possible power struggles.

Identify the purpose of this behavior and the beliefs that motivate it. If a member is challenging mainly to be the center of attention — "I belong only if others are involved with me" — you need to find a way to encourage the person by recognizing assets and contributions. But if the member is seeking power and control, you may need the assistance of the group to redirect the person. You could ask, "What seems to be happening in the group now?" or, "How do you feel about what Kirsty is saying?" If the members give feedback to the challenger and you move on, the problem is usually resolved.

You can also give some feedback to the challenger by saying something like, "This idea doesn't appeal to you." Then ask the person if what he is doing in the family is working. If the person says it's working, ask him to evaluate the costs of the current procedure. For example, you could ask, "When you . . . what is the child learning?" "Is that what you want the child to learn?" Then if the person begins to "see the light," ask the member if she or he is willing to experiment with the new idea.

If the person says what he or she is doing is not working, ask the person if she or he would be willing to experiment with the new idea to see what happens. If the person's willing, move on.

If the person is not willing to experiment with the new idea, again remind the person and the group of the freedom to accept or reject an idea. You could also ask if the person would be willing just to think about the idea.

Some people who challenge play the role of the expert. They've boned up on child rearing and marital relationships through reading other books, magazines, watching TV programs, whatever. This might be a very interesting intellectual discussion in a university class, but it's not the purpose of this group.

If this happens, you can ask the group what they think is happening: "What ground rule applies here?" (Stick to the topic). You can also say that the person may have a point, but that the group is organized to consider and discuss the ideas presented in *Calming the Family Storm*. Clarify that it's your job to help the group focus on what the book has to offer, not to debate other ideas.

Blaming. Some people are expert at blaming others for their problems. "If only he or she would . . . ." In effect these folks transfer the responsibility for their anger to others — kids, spouses, ex-spouses. Some blame factors at work — "I'm under so much pressure on the job." Others blame nature or a person's upbringing — "He was born that way." "It's the way her parents raised her."

Ask others what they think or what ground rule applies (Take responsibility for your choices). If necessary, reflect what the person is really saying: "It seems to me that you're saying nothing you do has any influence on your relationship with . . . ." Sometimes this is enough; the person recognizes her faulty belief. If not, you can tell the person that the purpose of the group is to help each participant decide what she can do, not what other family members should do. It's a matter of assuming responsibility for one's own behavior which puts one in a position to choose what to do about it.

Catastrophizing. There may be a person in your group who catastrophizes: "But what if this happens?" or "What do you do when . . . ?" The first thing to do is to determine whether the issue will be covered in a later session and say, "We'll cover that in session . . . ."

If the concern is not covered in a future session, ask if the person has ever experienced the concern. If the answer is yes, ask for a specific example. If the person hasn't experienced the concern but is worried that it might happen, then you can respond by saying that of course anything is possible, but it's best to work from actual experiences. You can also ask the group what they would do if such a thing happened.

If the behavior continues, the person may be looking for reasons not to change. You can say something like, "I get the feeling you're looking for reasons not to change your current procedures. If so, that's okay, it's up to you."

Monopolizing. Group members who monopolize may believe they must be the center of attention or be in control. They become concerned whenever they aren't the focus of the discussion.

Don't ask the group what they think is happening, because the monopolizer may feel attacked. The best strategy is to handle the problem yourself. You can lessen the influence of the monopolizer, by saying something like: "I'm getting concerned. If we continue to discuss this we're going to run out of time for other things that we need to discuss. Let's move on and if there's time later, we can come back to this." Then move on.

Since a person who monopolizes wants to be important, it can be helpful to give the person a task. Meet with the member and ask him or her to assist you in recalling what the group discusses in sessions. Would the person be willing to be a note-taker?

If the monopolization continues, you may have to have a private conversation with the group member and talk about the need to give everyone a chance to share. If the person feels he or she needs more focus, then perhaps individual or family counseling is the best approach.

Some monopolizers don't focus on their own issues, but monopolize by being the one who always gives opinions on the concepts in the book, or constantly gives others advice on their issues. If this is the case, you can redirect the discussion by asking others what they think about the issue.

"Yes, butting." People who "yes, but" are often communicating to you and the rest of the group that they have no intention of making any changes. By saying "Yes, but . . . , " or words to that effect, they intend only to impress the group with their good intentions — they dare not risk their image by saying no. They will say something like: "Well, I think that's a good idea, but . . . ," or "I'd like to do that, but . . ."

Ask the group what they think the member is really saying. If the group doesn't understand the meaning of the member's message, give your own impressions. "When you say, 'Yes, but . . . ,' I hear you saying, 'No, I really don't want to do that.' That's okay; we're not here to pressure you to do anything you don't want to do."

Of course some "yes, buts" can be legitimate when the person means the idea will work in one situation but not another, and the explanation makes sense. A person who continually says "yes, but," however, is most likely communicating that he or she is looking for reasons not to change.

A Word About Mandated Group Members

Mandated group members may be angry and resistant because they've been ordered to take a class. They may transfer this anger toward you as the leader. Applying what you're learning about resistance in this section can help defuse the anger and resistance. Of course, like anyone else, they are free to accept or reject the ideas. Rejecting the ideas could create consequences for them such as continued problems with the court and maybe losing their kids. But this is not your problem — they own it unless you suspect more child abuse, then you own the problem and need to report it.

Some mandated parents may be so frightened of losing their children that they are very anxious to learn anything they can, which may cause them to misapply the principles or try to apply too many new ideas at a time. This can create problems. The group can help such members understand the principles and prioritize the changes they make. They will need lots of encouragement as they attempt change.

Just like resistance, the misapplication of principles isn't restricted to just frightened mandated members. Some questions you can ask the group for any members who misapply the principles are: "What do you think will happen if Brian continues to . . . ?" "Does anyone else have a different interpretation of what the authors mean by . . . ?"

For those who want to change all at once, you can remind them of the ground rule or guideline "Have patience — change takes time." Ask the member or the group how the person can prioritize changes.

For mandated group members, whether they are resisters or frightened, it's best if they are in a mixed group — one with non-mandated members as well — people who take the class simply because they are interested in improving their family relationships and are not ordered to take an anger management class. These folks can be good models for mandated members. Running a group for just mandated people is extremely challenging and can be discouraging.

In a mixed group, only you and the mandated members should know they are mandated — this is their personal business, not the business of the rest of the group. Some mandated people will want to share this fact — this is their choice. This can happen when you're assessing the goals of the group, when you ask "What do you want to learn from this experience?" or as they become more comfortable in the group.

Now that you've discovered what I consider an appropriate leadership role, skills and what to do with problem members, you're ready to run your group. In Part 5, "Session Format — How to Organize Each Session," I'll discuss the sections of the lesson plan.

PART 5

Session Format —
How to Organize Each Session

The following format allows the group members to understand and apply the material and to learn from interaction with each other and the leader.

At the end of each session, "Action Steps" — concepts and skills for the group members to apply based on the discussion of the reading assignment for the session — are assigned. Beginning with the second session, ask members to report their experience with applying the Action Steps assigned in the last session. Reading for the next session is also assigned at this time. (NOTE: You may want to write the Action Steps and Reading Assignment on a handout. The handout could be given at the end of each session, or you could include the assignments for all sessions on a handout and distribute it in the first session.)

SESSION FORMAT

REPORTS

Review the assigned Action Steps (See Part 6, "Study Guide — Chapter by Chapter"), with the group, and ask: "Who would like to share their experience with applying these steps?" (NOTE: Journaling is introduced in chapter 3: "How We Create Our Anger." Reporting can involve members reading an entry in their journal.)

Members who may have experienced difficulty in applying the suggestions may be asked to describe the situation. Explore with the group the possible reasons for the problem. Encourage the member to apply the concept this week with the new understanding.

CHAPTERS DISCUSSION

You could begin the discussion with members sharing any comments they have written down. Review the "Major Points" for each chapter, then continue the discussion with the following open-ended questions as needed. Ask members to share their own examples for questions 2 and 3.

1. What did you learn from the reading?
2. What ideas in the reading were particularly helpful? Why?

3. How would you apply the ideas in the chapters to your family?
4. Any questions about the reading?

If you've developed your own questions to bring out points you want to emphasize, you could follow the sharing of comments and/or general questions with your specific questions, asking members to give their own examples in response to your questions. (NOTE: There are also specific questions and directions in Part 6, "Study Guide — Chapter by Chapter." Use some of the specific questions and directions to discuss certain concepts, elicit examples, and practice skills.)

SUMMARY OF THE SESSION

Ask the group to summarize the session, telling what they learned. You could ask: "What did you learn in this session?" Or poll the group by asking each member to state one thing she or he learned in the session. Clear up any misconceptions.

ASSIGNMENTS FOR THE NEXT SESSION

Action Steps: Suggest the members apply the book's suggestions discussed in this session — the Action Steps. (See Part 6)

Reading Assignment: Assign the chapters for the next session.

Encourage the group to keep journaling.

CONCLUDING THE CLASS

After summarizing your last session, you could conclude your class in the following manner: Ask them to give their impressions of the class. You could ask:
1. "What did you gain from this class?"
2. "If you feel the class could be improved, what suggestions do you have?"

You could ask the group to respond to these questions in writing if there is time. A written evaluation will be helpful in planning your next class.

Encourage members to apply any of the concepts in chapters 15, 16, and 17 that relate to their own special situations regarding divorce, single parenting, stepfamilies, family violence, apologies and forgiveness. Ask them to continue to apply the other ideas they've learned from reading the book and class discussion. (NOTE: You may want to suggest a "check-up" session in a few weeks to see how things are going. If members would like to do this, set a date and time.)

In Part 6, "Study Guide — Chapter by Chapter," the Major Points, specific questions and directions and action steps are listed for each chapter.

PART 6

Study Guide —
Chapter by Chapter

This Study Guide provides the following information for each chapter of *Calming the Family Storm*:

- **Major Points:** reminders of the concepts (for your convenience so you don't have to flip through the text);
- **Specific Questions and Directions** should the general questions or comments from the group fail to generate a productive discussion, and
- **Action Steps:** assignments for applying the concepts and skills they are learning.

Due to limited time, you won't be able to use all the questions and directions for each chapter, so choose those which cover content you want to emphasize and that you think the group might have missed. If there is misunderstanding of certain concepts, reading those portions of the book aloud in the session can be helpful.

CHAPTER 1: "ONE BIG HAPPY FAMILY . . . OR IS IT?" (PP. 1–10)

MAJOR POINTS
- Anger is a normal emotion that we all experience. We can calm the family storm by learning to manage anger well.
- Effective anger management in the family requires equality and mutual respect.
- The stress of life today contributes to anger in our families.
- Technology has taught us to expect immediate results. Anger often follows unfulfilled expectations.
- The impact of the democratic revolution accounts for much of the anger and conflict in today's families. It is a major reason that family relationships must be founded on mutual respect to succeed.
- Angry parents can frighten children, increase rebellion and revenge and teach them that cooperation is only required when someone is angry with them (if they decide to cooperate at all!).

- Anger can result in domestic violence and child abuse. If you or your children are victims of abuse, this book alone is not sufficient. *Get professional help.*

Specific Questions and Directions

1. Why is there so much anger in families? (pp. 5–7)
2. What are some of the stresses you experience which may lead to anger?
3. How does anger affect your family relationships? (pp. 7–8)

Action Steps

No action steps in this chapter as it is an introductory chapter.

◆ ◆ ◆

Chapter 2: "The Anatomy of Anger" (pp. 11–26)

Major Points

- For people who feel inadequate, threatened and powerless, anger can be a form of protest, a way to feel temporarily powerful.
- Anger is a "fight or flight" reaction to situations where we fear our survival is threatened.
- Emotions do not "just happen." You create most of your anger by your beliefs and interpretation of events.
- Among the many myths about anger: humans are naturally aggressive; holding anger is dangerous to your health; expressing anger is cathartic; acting out anger gets rid of it.
- Anger — like all emotions — is neither "good" nor "bad"; it depends on how the emotion is used.
- Anger can act as a "warning device," telling you that something is wrong — in yourself or in your relationship — and needs to be addressed.
- You can't always choose what happens to you but you do have choices about how you interpret what happens.
- You make yourself angry by "angry thinking" or "hot thoughts" — judging; catastrophizing; "can't-standing"; demanding; blaming.
- Anger often comes from the "MADS": Minimizing your personal power; Awfulizing or catastrophizing; Demanding; Shaming and blaming.
- Anger expression may be a "power move," to gain control, win, get even, or protect rights.

◆ Anger is often related to fear, anxiety, stress, guilt, depression, annoyance, hurt, frustration, disappointment, or other emotions. Look carefully for the source of your anger.

SPECIFIC QUESTIONS AND DIRECTIONS

1. Who is responsible for your anger? (pp. 12–13)
2. What are the "Anger Facts and Fictions"? (pp. 13–14)
3. What does the acronym "MADS" stand for? How could you use this model to help you understand your angry beliefs or "hot thoughts"? (pp. 16–17)
4. What are the purposes of anger? What are some examples of the negative uses of control? Positive uses? Negative uses of winning? Positive uses of winning? How can you protect your rights or the rights of your children without using anger? Why is getting even always negative? How can you get yourself out of desiring revenge? (pp. 17–19)
5. What is a "challenge-based" emotion? (pp. 19–22) What are some "challenge-based" emotions you experience along with your anger? (You could refer to the chart on page 25, "Feelings That Often Go with Anger" for examples of challenge-based emotions.)
6. What is the relationship between guilt and anger? What are the purposes of guilt? How can you rid yourself of guilt feelings? (pp. 22–23)
7. What is the relationship between stress and anger?
8. What are some positive ways to manage your stress? (pp. 23–24)

ACTION STEPS

1. Begin to examine at your beliefs — "hot thoughts" and MADS — and purposes when you are angry. (pp. 15–19)
2. Search for other emotions associated with your anger — the "challenge-based" feelings such as guilt and stress. (pp. 22–24) You can also use the chart on page 25 to help you identify "The Feelings That Often Go with Anger."

◆ ◆ ◆

CHAPTER 3: "ANGER MANAGEMENT STRATEGIES I — FIRST STEPS" (PP. 27–35)

MAJOR POINTS

- Anger management begins by recognizing your "storm warnings" — triggers and body language.
- Triggers — "hot spots" — are situations or behavior of others that invite or stimulate your anger.
- Body language can tell you that you're "heating up," and can communicate your anger to others. Pay attention to it.
- When you're feeling angry, you have three choices: suppress it (don't: you'll go over and over it later), express it (be careful: you may produce an unwanted confrontation), or reassess it (good choice: change your thinking and behavior about the situation).
- Interrupt your anger on the spot: avoid your first impulse; walk away; tell yourself calming phrases; count to 10; visualize; tell yourself to "Stop, Think and Act."
- Consciously decide whether or not to express your anger. Will it clear the air or make things worse? Consider how the other person will feel and react.
- Rate your anger. Is it worth it — on a scale of 1–10 — to express your anger in this situation?

SPECIFIC QUESTIONS AND DIRECTIONS

1. What are some of your anger triggers or "hot spots"? How does your body tell you and/or others that you're "heating up"? (Go over chart on pages 30–31, "Storm Warnings: Anger Triggers/Body Language.")
2. What are some ways to interrupt your anger on the spot? (pp. 29, 32–34) What is the Stop, Think and Act technique? (p. 33) How can you use the technique to manage your anger?
3. How do you decide whether or not to express your anger? (pp. 33–34)
4. How can rating your anger help you manage it? (p. 34)

ACTION STEPS

1. Examine your triggers and body language by completing the chart on pages 30–31, "Storm Warnings: Anger Trigger/Body Language."
2. Experiment with the "Techniques to Interrupt Your Anger on the Spot." (pp. 29, 32–34)

◆ ◆ ◆

Chapter 4: "Anger Management Strategies II — For the Long Term" (pp. 36–48)

Major Points

- Long-term anger management takes time. Get started by writing down your hot thoughts.
- Examine your "MADS." (Minimizing, Awfulizing, Demanding, Shaming)
- Examine the purpose of your anger in a situation: Control, win, get even, or protect your rights.
- Create "cool" thoughts: You can handle unpleasant situations; this isn't a catastrophe; "your wishes are not the other person's command."
- Reassess your purpose: (For example: You can control your anger; you can't control the other person.)
- Reframe the situation: What's another way to look at this?
- Find the humor: There must be something funny in all this.
- Don't revisit past hurts and failures; do revisit past successes.
- Look at it from the other person's view.
- Talk it over with a third party or spiritual guide.
- Exercise away the tension you experience when you're angry or stressed.
- Minimize or eliminate the use of alcohol and other drugs.
- List things to do about your anger.
- Practice deep breathing, relaxation, and visualization.

Specific Questions and Directions

1. What do the authors mean by "dispute your irrational 'hot' thoughts and purposes"? (pp. 36–39) (Ask for an example and lead group through the disputing process using the "MADS" and disputing thoughts and purposes. The example could come from journal sharing.)
2. What is meant by "cool" thoughts? (pp. 39–40) (Use the example from the group discussed in question 1 to go through the process of creating cool thoughts and positive purposes.)
3. Discuss the "Other Techniques for Managing Anger." (pp. 41–47) Discuss how each technique could be applied to the example being discussed.
4. Take the group through the deep breathing and relaxation exercise on pages 45–46, and the visualization and self-talk exercise on pages 46–47.

ACTION STEPS

1. Use information on pages 37–40 to help you analyze and dispute your "hot" thoughts (MADS) and purposes, and create "cool" thoughts and positive purposes.

2. Experiment with some of the "Other Techniques for Managing Anger" to help you create cool thoughts. (pp. 41–47)

◆ ◆ ◆

CHAPTER 5: "FIVE STEPS TO LESS ANGER IN YOUR LIFE" (PP. 49–61)

MAJOR POINTS

◆ *Step 1: Examine the anger-provoking situation:* What happened? How did you respond? What were the consequences of your action? How angry were you?

◆ *Step 2: Examine your inner processes — your MADS:* How are you Minimizing personal power? How are you Awfulizing? How are you Demanding? How are you Shaming and blaming?

◆ *Step 3: Rethink the situation.* Is it really true that you can't stand it? That it's a catastrophe? That it must be different? That the other person is bad, rotten, worthless?

◆ *Step 4: Create "cool thoughts" and a positive purpose.* You can stand it. It's frustrating but not awful. Your demands are really wishes. The person is okay, even if the behavior is not. Change your purpose to controlling the situation or yourself, not the other person. Work for the win-win. Make things fair, not even. Protect your rights without anger.

◆ *Step 5: Choose to change your own behavior, and follow through.* What changes will you make to improve the relationship? Act on your decision, don't just "try" to do it.

Use the 5 steps to deal with your self-anger as well as your anger toward others.

SPECIFIC QUESTIONS AND DIRECTIONS

1. Go over the 5 Steps on pages 50–55 and apply the steps to a shared journal example.

2. Go over the chart "My Anger Journal: Five Steps for Managing Anger" on page 60, and encourage the group to set up their journal in this manner and to continue journaling.

Use the "Five Steps to Less Anger in Your Life" in chapter 5 and write down your answers to the questions about anger incidents. (pp. 50–55) Set up your journal using the chart "My Anger Journal: Five Steps for Managing Anger" on page 60.

◆ ◆ ◆

Chapter 6: "Encouraging Relationships" (pp. 62-85)

Major Points

- ◆ Encouragement means building courage and self-esteem in yourself and your family members.

- ◆ Encouragement says "I believe in you, I appreciate you, I recognize your effort, I celebrate your accomplishments, and I am on your side."

- ◆ If you're frequently angry with family members, you may be engaged in power contests, trying to win, control or get even.

- ◆ The democratic revolution has changed relationships and social institutions to an "equality identity," so each person can say, "I am not inferior, I have equal value, I deserve respect."

- ◆ Real change in a relationship becomes possible when each person lets go of trying to change the other, and focuses attention on her role and what she can contribute.

- ◆ A new "golden rule" for couples: "Do unto my partner as my partner wishes to have done unto her/him" (as long as it's mutually respectful).

- ◆ Discouraging parenting style I: The Coercive Parenting Style — controlling children "for their own good." The model for this style is *limits without freedom.*

- ◆ Discouraging parenting style II: The Pampering or Permissive Parenting Style — making children comfortable and happy by indulging them (pampering) or letting them do whatever they please (permissiveness). The model for this style is *freedom without limits.*

- ◆ Encouraging parenting style: Respectful Leadership — exhibits mutual respect, firmness, and kindness. The model for this style is *freedom within limits.*

- ◆ Encouragement skills include: accepting; instilling faith and confidence; building on strengths; accentuating the positive; and promoting responsibility.

- ◆ Praise and encouragement are not the same. Praise is a reward based on accomplishment. Encouragement accepts people and promotes self- and people-esteem.

◆ Encouragement must underlie everything you do with your family members if you're to build positive relationships and foster cooperation.

Specific Questions and Directions

1. How do the authors describe encouragement? (pp. 62–64) How can you use encouragement in your family relationships?

2. What is meant by the "democratic revolution"? How do the authors define equality? (pp. 64–65)

3. What role does anger play in the transition from autocratic to democratic relationships? How has the democratic revolution impacted couple relationships? Parent-child relationships? (pp. 64–67)

4. What is meant by "A New Golden Rule" for couples?" (pp. 67–70) How could you apply this to your relationship?

5. If you are a single parent, and you're not in a supportive relationship, how could you build such a relationship? (p. 70)

6. The authors describe two discouraging parenting styles: coercive and pampering or permissive. What characterizes the coercive parenting style? Pampering or permissive style? (pp. 71–74) How do these styles apply to your relationship with your children?

7. The authors describe respectful leadership as an encouraging parenting style. How does this style differ from the discouraging coercive and pampering or permissive styles? (p. 74) How could you apply this style to your relationship with your kids?

8. The authors describe five encouragement skills: accepting; instilling faith and confidence; building on strengths; accentuating the positive; and promoting responsibility. How could you apply these skills to your family? (p. 74–78) To yourself? (pp. 83–84)

9. What is the difference between praise and encouragement? (pp. 78-80, 82) (Go over the chart on page 81.)

10. My Personal Encourager Exercise (p. 83). Divide the group into dyads to do the exercise. (Note, if you're short on time, make it an individual homework assignment.)

11. What is meant by "an encouraging attitude"? (p. 82) How could you establish an encouraging attitude in your family?

1. Apply the "New Golden Rule for Couples" if you're in a couple relationship or a single parent in a relationship. (pp. 67–70) If you're not in a relationship, use some of the ideas for building a support system. (p. 70)

2. Examine your parenting style and begin working toward an encouraging "Respectful Leadership" style. (pp. 71–74, 83–84)

3. Apply the encouragement skills to your family members and yourself: accepting; instilling faith and confidence; building on strengths; accentuating the positive; and promoting responsibility. (pp. 74–78)

4. Do the "My Personal Encourager" exercise on page 83 (if it's not done in class).

◆ ◆ ◆

CHAPTER 7: "HEALTHY COMMUNICATION" (PP. 86–112)

MAJOR POINTS

- Anger in relationships is often fueled by misunderstandings and lack of good communication.

- Listening — "receiving" — involves really hearing how a person feels; doing your best to understand the emotions behind the words, tone of voice and body language.

- Listening begins with making a connection by inviting the other person to talk about his or her feelings.

- Reflective listening (restating what you understand the person to be saying and why) helps make it clear that you understand both his feelings and the content of his story.

- *Reflective listening* can help both when family members are upset and when they feel good about something.

- When communicating your feelings — "sending" — avoid "you-messages," which attack, blame or put down the other person: "You're a jerk! You make me so mad!"

- Express your feelings effectively with "I-messages," which convey that you take responsibility for your feelings: "When [something happens], I feel [angry, sad, frustrated . . .] because [how it affects you]."

- Adding an "I'd appreciate" statement, if your I-message goes unheeded, lets the person know what she can do to rectify the situation in the future.

- Whether or not to express your anger depends upon whether you think the expression will influence a positive change or make things worse.

- Some will respond positively to direct expression of anger, others will not. You may choose instead to express the feelings associated with anger, such as frustration, fear or hurt.
- The more positive feelings you share as I-messages, the more encouraging you are and the greater your chances of gaining cooperation with the important people in your life.
- The "Heart to Heart" communication model can reduce "vertical communication," increase "level communication," and increase intimacy, through connection and mutual understanding.
- Couples can schedule a "heart to heart" session once a week, listening to each other without judgment, and sharing feelings in a respectful way.
- The "heart to heart" model works well with children also, on a regular basis, one-to-one, sharing feelings with mutual respect and without judgment.

SPECIFIC QUESTIONS AND DIRECTIONS

1. The authors list several listening or receiving skills on pages 86–88. (Ask the group to locate the skills in the book.) How could you apply these skills to your family?

2. What is reflective listening? What is a simple formula for making a reflective listening response? What are some other ways to form a reflective listening response? (pp. 88–90) Discuss the practice examples on page 90. Have the group give responses to the examples. If there's time, use an example from the group and practice a reflective listening dialogue such as the ones on pages 91–92.

3. Why is it important to reflect pleasant feelings as well as unpleasant ones? (pp. 92–93)

4. What is the difference between a "you-message" and an "I-message"? Why are I-messages more effective? How do you form an I-message? (pp. 94–97) When using an I-message, why is it important to avoid the word "you" whenever possible? (p. 96)

5. When is it appropriate to add an "I'd appreciate" statement? (p. 97) (Have a member give an example where an I-message would be appropriate, and form the I-message, including an "I'd appreciate" statement.)

6. How do you decide whether it's better to use an I-message to express your anger directly or an I-message to express the challenge-based emotion associated with your anger? (pp. 98–100) (If there's time, go over practice situations on pages 101–102 and ask the group to provide responses.)

7. Why is it also important to use I-messages to express your pleasant feelings? (pp. 102–103) Ask the group to give examples of using I-messages to express their pleasant feelings.

8. On pages 103–105, examples are given for using reflective listening and I-messages together. If there's time, have the group give their own examples of situations from their families and role play using I-messages and reflective listening together.

9. What is "Heart to Heart Communication for Couples"? What are the benefits of this model? How could you apply this model to your couple relationship?

10. How could you apply the "Heart to Heart Communication" model to your relationship with your children? (pp. 105–110)

ACTION STEPS

Use "receiving skills" such as reflective listening and respectful "sending skills" — I-messages—in your communication with family members. (pp. 86–106)

◆ ◆ ◆

CHAPTER 8: "PROBLEM SOLVING AND CONFLICT RESOLUTION" (PP. 113–130)

MAJOR POINTS

- ◆ Problems and conflict are inevitable in relationships, but they can be lessened and resolved.
- ◆ Reflective listening and I-messages are very helpful in problem solving discussions.
- ◆ Helpful tools for problem solving also include recognizing who owns the problem and finding solutions by exploring alternatives.
- ◆ Encouragement — accepting the person, instilling confidence, building on strengths, accentuating the positive, promoting responsibility — is important for effective problem solving.
- ◆ If another family member owns the problem and wants to talk it over, you can listen and help her explore alternatives. The decision on what to do is up to her (unless it's dangerous).
- ◆ If you the problem, you help brainstorm solutions and have a major say in choosing the solution.
- ◆ Common mistakes in conflict resolution: problem solving when angry; focusing on who's right and who's wrong; believing you must agree on all important matters; focusing on the past; ignoring the future.

- Conflicts are often signs of disrespect: anger, name-calling, or punitive silence. The first step in resolving conflicts is to establish mutual respect.

- The issue people fight about may not be the real issue; it's the topic of the conflict. Real issues involve who's right, who's in control, who's going to win, who's superior.

- There is agreement in a conflict — the parties have agreed to fight! To change the agreement, decide what you are willing to do, not what the other person must do.

SPECIFIC QUESTIONS AND DIRECTIONS

1. What is meant by "who owns the problem"? How do you determine who owns the problem? (pp. 113–114) Go over "Examples of Problem Ownership" chart on page 115 and ask the group to share their own examples.

2. What can you do when another family member owns the problem? When you own the problem? (pp. 114–115)

3. What is meant by "exploring alternatives"? What are the four steps to the exploring alternatives process? What is the value of encouragement in problem solving discussions? (pp. 116–118)

4. How can you provide assistance when a family member owns the problem? (118–19) How can you use exploring alternatives to negotiate when you own the problem? (pp. 123–124)

5. Go over the "Problem Solving Through Exploring Alternatives" chart on page 118 to help the group understand the differences in how the process is applied to provide assistance or to negotiate.

6. What are the principles of conflict resolution? (p. 124) What are some common mistakes for people in conflict? (Refer group to the sidebar on pages 122–23.)

7. If there's time, have the group role play using exploring alternatives to provide assistance, and to negotiate.

ACTION STEPS

1. Decide who owns the problem. Use the guidelines on pages 113–115 to determine problem ownership and what you can do based on who owns the problem.

2. Use the exploring alternatives process when appropriate to help family members if they desire assistance in solving a problem they own. Use the process for conflict resolution when appropriate for problems you own. Review pages 116–129 for guidelines on when to use exploring alternatives and the steps of exploring alternatives.

◆ ◆ ◆

Chapter 9: "Family and Couple Meetings" (pp. 131–144)

Major Points

- Regularly scheduled meetings in the family give members a recognized forum in which to make plans and bring up issues.
- Topics for family meetings include problem solving, making plans, discussions on how to share chores, and planning family fun.
- Not all family issues are appropriate for children's input. If their ideas and feelings are heard, however, kids feel valued.
- Between meetings, family members need a way to post issues on the agenda for discussion at the next meeting.
- Rotate leadership roles for each family meeting, as age-appropriate: leader, time keeper, and secretary or note-taker.
- Decisions should be evaluated for several weeks and fine-tuned or changed if not working.
- A weekly couple meeting gives partners a designated time to work on issues that do not involve the children and to bring quality time — and fun — to their relationship.

Specific Questions and Directions

1. Why is it important to hold family meetings? What kinds of issues can family meetings deal with? Why is it important to include planning family fun in family meetings? (pp. 131, 134–136)
2. Go over the sidebar "Leadership Skills for Family Meetings" on pages 132–133.
3. Why is it important that decisions reached in a family meeting be in effect only until the next meeting? (pp. 135–136)
4. How do couple meetings differ from family meetings? What are the benefits of couple meetings? (pp. 140–141)

Action Steps

Begin family meetings and couple meetings (if you are in a couple relationship and your partner agrees) this week, following the guidelines on pages 131–136 and 140–141.

◆ ◆ ◆

CHAPTER 10: "ALL'S FAIR IN LOVE . . ." (PP. 145–163)

MAJOR POINTS

♦ Mutual respect is essential if relationships are to thrive long term.

♦ Twelve Principles for Couples: (1) Make the relationship a priority, (2) Take responsibility for your part in the relationship, (3) Maintain mutual respect and social equality, (4) Support individuality for yourself and your partner, (5) Have fun together, (6) Develop a balanced and mutually agreed-upon division of labor, (7) Encourage one another, (8) Communicate effectively, (9) Solve problems together, (10) Understand and correct your own belief system, (11) Understand, empathize with and respond to your partner's belief system, (12) Express respectful affection and intimacy.

♦ Experiences and beliefs from the past — "hot spots" — are likely to impact the present. Watch carefully if anger increases for no obvious reason. This is a time to reflect on what issue from the past you are bringing into the present.

♦ When you and your partner can pinpoint your hot spots, you can catch yourself and make other choices before anger erupts.

SPECIFIC QUESTIONS AND DIRECTIONS

1. Go over the "Twelve Principles for Effective Couple Relationships." (pp. 147–154) Ask members who are in a couple relationship for examples of how they can apply the principles.

2. Go over the section "How a Couple's Beliefs Impact Their Relationship." (pp. 157–161) Ask for examples from members who are in couple relationship to share how their beliefs or "hot spots" affect their relationship.

ACTION STEPS

Complete the "Twelve Principles Inventory" (p. 156) and the "Belief Systems Exercise" (p. 162) and share results with each other if you're in a couple relationship and your partner agrees.

CHAPTER 11: "DISCIPLINE WITHOUT ANGER" (PP. 164–76)

MAJOR POINTS

♦ Our kids are part of the "democratic revolution" in human relationships. Traditional autocratic methods of discipline don't work very well.

♦ Effective discipline does not include punishment, which is most often ineffective.

♦ Punishment is usually administered by frustrated, angry parents. Any cooperation derived from punishment is often short-lived.

- Parents who rely on rewards are giving this message: "You should expect to be paid for good behavior."
- Instead of the desired result, kids may see rewards as something they are entitled to.
- Kids may attempt to achieve a sense of belonging through misbehavior if they find cooperation doesn't work.
- Misbehavior has purpose: attention, power, revenge, or displaying inadequacy.
- Redirect your child's goal and misbehavior by examining your own belief, purpose and behavior. Change "hot thoughts" to "cool thoughts" and develop a positive purpose.

SPECIFIC QUESTIONS AND DIRECTIONS

1. What is the meaning of discipline? (p. 165)
2. What are the pitfalls of punishment? (p. 165) Why are rewards often unrewarding?
3. Why do children misbehave? (p. 166)
4. What are the four goals of misbehavior? (Go over each goal to make sure the group understands the concepts.) (pp. 167–171)
5. Which goals relate to anger? What is happening when a child displays inadequacy — the fourth goal? (p. 169)
6. How do you discover what goal your child is seeking by a particular misbehavior? (pp. 169, 171) (Go over Chart 1: "The Four Goals of Misbehavior" on page 170.)
7. What do parents typically tell themselves when their child seeks attention? Power? Revenge? When the child is displaying inadequacy? How can you change your self-talk when your child seeks attention? Power? Revenge? When the child is displaying inadequacy? (pp. 171–175)
8. Go over Chart 2: "Points of Conflict (and Collaboration) Between Parent and Child" on page 175.

ACTION STEPS

1. Identify the goal of misbehavior when your child is misbehaving using the guidelines on pages 166–171.
2. Examine your belief, purpose and behavior in response to the goal of a particular misbehavior you experience with your child. Change your "hot thoughts" to "cool thoughts," develop a positive purpose and change your behavioral response to the child so that you don't reinforce the misbehavior but, instead, redirect the child's goal and misbehavior. (pp. 171–175)

◆ ◆ ◆

Chapter 12: "Children's Choices and Consequences" (pp. 177–195)

Major Points

◆ The more choices you give, the more opportunities kids have to learn to make good decisions.

◆ Give kids choices — within the limits of age and abilities — and allow them to experience the consequences — positive or negative, depending on the choices they make.

◆ There are two types of consequences: natural and logical.

◆ A natural consequence results when we allow the laws of nature to take their course, or comes from experiencing the "natural flow of events" . . . without interference from us.

◆ Logical consequences are created by parents when a natural consequence is dangerous or there is no natural consequence for a particular misbehavior.

◆ To be effective, the consequence must fit the misbehavior. The child may not like the results, but they make sense to the child.

◆ Don't respond to children's griping, complaints and promises to behave better. Use "on the spot" anger management techniques to keep yourself from responding.

◆ Use consequences as an opportunity for your child to learn to make good decisions, not as a substitute for punishment, or in a punitive way.

◆ Logical consequences focus on cooperation, are logically related to the misbehavior, separate the deed from the doer, focus on the present, show respect for the child, and give choices.

◆ When using consequences, identify the child's goal of misbehavior, consider who owns the problem, and don't talk too much.

Specific Questions and Directions

1. Why is it important to give kids choices? (pp. 177–178)
2. What are natural consequences? (pp. 178–180) Ask the group to share examples with their kids which are appropriate for natural consequences.
3. What is a logical consequence? (pp. 180–182) Ask the group to share situations with their kids where logical consequences would apply.
4. Why is your attitude and intention important when using natural or logical consequences? (pp. 181–182)
5. Go over the chart "Differences Between Punishment and Logical Consequences" on page 183.

6. What is the purpose of time-out? How can you use time-out effectively? (pp. 182, 184)

7. Go over "Consequences and the Typical Daily Routine" on pages 184–192 and 194. Ask the group for any questions they have about the suggested consequences for the misbehaviors discussed in the section. Ask the group: Which of these consequences will you apply with your kids?

8. Go over the sidebar "Things to Consider When Using Consequences" on pages 192–193. Ask: Why is it important to identify the child's goal of misbehavior? To consider who owns the problem? To avoid talking too much?

ACTION STEPS

Replace reward and punishment for discipline challenges with natural and logical consequences. Follow the guidelines for natural and logical consequences on pages 177–184 and pages 192–193. (If you face challenges in your family's daily routine, experiment with some of the suggestions on pages 184-191 and page 194.)

◆ ◆ ◆

CHAPTER 13: "WHEN KIDS GET ANGRY" (PP. 196–213)

MAJOR POINTS

- ◆ When your child is angry at you: don't do what the child expects; Stop, Think and Act; consider your child's goal; force yourself to think of something else; ignore the behavior; use reflective listening and problem solving; move away from the child; remove the child to a time-out area.

- ◆ Don't overreact to sibling conflicts. Your attention may be the reason they continue!

- ◆ Parental hot spots are often activated by sibling conflict: family alliances; biological alliances; birth order identification; gender identification; lack of protection in childhood.

- ◆ Let kids work it out by themselves whenever possible. Intervene only when necessary for safety, and then take a neutral position.

- ◆ Ask, who owns the problem? When siblings argue or scuffle, it's their problem. They created it, and they own the responsibility to solve it.

- ◆ If a dispute involves a toy or other object, or a house guest, a logical consequence will apply. Stop fighting over the object, or lose use of it. The house guest can go home.

- If your rights are being violated, or safety or property is at risk, you own the problem and the solution is up to you.

- When a child tattles, you can: use reflective listening, explore alternatives with the tattler or tell the tattler to bring it up at the family meeting. If safety or illegal behavior is involved, you own the problem and have a responsibility to address it.

SPECIFIC QUESTIONS AND DIRECTIONS

1. Why is it important to avoid your first impulse when your child is angry with you? What are some other things you can do when your child is angry with you? (pp. 196–198)

2. In sibling conflicts, why do younger siblings try to get the older ones in trouble? (pp. 199–200) Ask the group to share any examples they have of sibling conflict.

3. What are some common parental "hot spots" activated when their kids get into fights and arguments? (pp. 200–202) Which of these "hot spots" fit for you?

4. What are the advantages of letting kids work out their own conflicts? (pp. 202–203) When and how should you get involved in sibling conflicts? (pp. 203–204)

5. What is the purpose of tattling? What are some ways to deal effectively with tattling? If the "tattling" involves safety or illegal issues, what can you do? (pp. 207–209)

6. How can you handle your kids' fights with friends or with kids in the neighborhood? When should you step in and how? (pp. 209–212)

ACTION STEPS

1. Use some of the techniques suggested for when your child is angry at you. (pp. 196–198)

2. Examine your "hot spots" regarding conflicts between your children. (pp. 200–202).

3. Let the kids work out their conflicts unless a child's safety, property or your rights are involved. (pp. 202–207)

4. Respond to tattling as suggested on pages 207–209.

5. Handle any peer conflicts as suggested on pages 209–212.

◆ ◆ ◆

Chapter 14: "Anger Management for Kids" (pp. 214–228)

Major Points

- Parents are the most influential people in the lives of their children, and are constantly teaching them how to interact and solve problems with others.

- Anger modeled by parents and observed by their children becomes natural and familiar, the method of choice for dealing with life's disappointments, stressors, and conflicts.

- Angry kids need a sounding board, a relationship with someone who really listens and educates, and does not judge or blame, so they can understand and handle their feelings.

- Teach kids about anger. E.g., anger is a natural human emotion; anger if expressed in hurtful ways causes problems in relationships; adults and kids alike are able to choose how to express anger; anger can be expressed in ways that are healthy for everyone.

- Use a variety of ways to teach kids to effectively manage anger: "What bugs me the most" lists; hot thoughts and cool thoughts; cool images; "on the spot" alternatives to acting out anger; TV as a teaching tool; role-playing and puppets; family meetings.

Specific Questions and Directions

1. When dealing with your kids, why is your model of anger management so important? (pp. 215–216)
2. When kids are angry, why is listening important? What are some situations where listening is inappropriate and why? (p. 218)
3. What do kids need to learn about anger? (pp. 218–220) What are some ways you can teach your kids about anger management? (Go over the suggested activities on pages 220–225.)
4. On pages 226–227 the authors suggest ways to help boys and girls with their anger. What are the differences in the suggestions for helping boys and for helping girls with their anger?

Action Steps

Use some of the techniques suggested in chapter 14 to teach your kids about anger management. (pp. 218-227)

◆ ◆ ◆

Chapter 15: "Angry Divorces, Single Parents, Stepfamilies" (pp. 229–260)

Major Points

- Children benefit tremendously when their divorced parents find a way to work out their relationship respectfully and cooperatively.

- Important steps to recover from a divorce: take time; create a support network; journal; examine your belief system; keep your conflicts in check; move on; consider how you will handle your ex-spouse's anger; consider professional help.

- If you sincerely believe that your children's safety is at risk as a result of your ex-spouse's behavior, legal action must be taken.

- If you are struggling with your own mental health and cannot adequately care for your children, seek the support of family members, professionals, and the relevant agencies in the community.

- Avoid criticizing, blaming, or condemning your ex-spouse in front of your children; don't use your children as messengers between you and your former spouse; reassure your children that they are loved, that the divorce is not their fault, and that they have value; support your children's relationship with both parents; focus your attention on your own relationship with the kids, don't try to control you ex's relationship with them; resist the temptation to make it up to them; understand your children's desire to live with both parents; don't let the kids act as your caretaker; pay your child support if it's your responsibility; maintain stability and routine; get professional help if needed.

- Recognize that single parents are capable of raising healthy and happy kids.

- Don't try to be both mother and father. You are one parent, one parent is all you can be, and one parent can do a fine job raising kids.

- Take care of yourself. Take time for doing the kinds of things that are restorative. Establish a support network.

- Help your kids to feel needed. Being counted on to do one's share of the household tasks adds to the feeling of being important and needed. Plus, you can use their help!

- Use family meetings to and work out differences, solve problems, develop plans, and encourage each other.

- Stepfamilies face many challenges and feelings that invite anger: grief and loss; confusing relationships; unrealistic expectations; loyalty issues; changing living conditions.

- Making a stepfamily is a process that takes time and patience. Celebrate the new, and allow ample time to grieve what's been left behind.

- Don't expect a new partner to be everything the divorced partner was not. Allow room for human imperfection.

- Parents often expect their spouse's biological children to love and accept them as a mom or a dad. A new relationship between stepparent and stepchild must be built over time.

- Accept that your feelings toward your own children will be different from those you have toward your stepchildren. As your relationship with your stepchildren grows and develops, so also will your feelings toward them.

- Resist the tendency to see your own children as always good or right and your stepchildren as bad or wrong (or vice versa). Stay out of the conflicts between the children whenever possible. Let them work it out.

- There is much to work out in stepfamilies, including relationships, rules, roles, chores, conflicts, and plans. Build in family meetings right from the beginning.

SPECIFIC QUESTIONS AND DIRECTIONS

1. What divorce issues invite anger? (pp. 231–232) (You may want to ask divorced group members what divorce issues are especially challenging for them.)
2. Review the authors' ideas for divorce recovery on pages 232–235.
3. Review the ideas for helping kids recover from divorce on pages 237–242.
4. Call the group's attention to the sidebar: "Make Your Children's Safety Your Number One Priority" on page 237. Ask: What are some issues that put children's safety at risk? What could you do if your child is at risk?
5. What are some of the challenges facing single parents? What are some common misconceptions about single parent households? (pp. 243–247)
6. Review the suggestions for single parents on pages 247–253.
7. Review the ideas for making stepfamilies work on pages 253–256.

ACTION STEPS

Apply the concepts in chapter 15 that relate to your situations regarding divorce, single parenting, or stepfamilies.

◆ ◆ ◆

Chapter 16: "When Anger Turns to Violence" (pp. 261–275)

Major Points

- Anger can turn to violence. When this occurs, a heavy toll is taken on individual and family mental health, which may impact family members for generations.

- Family violence doesn't end naturally; it has a definable cycle that escalates over time, and ends only through outside support and intervention — or a death.

- Domestic violence and child abuse are so serious and overwhelming to our sensibilities that a typical response is to minimize or deny their existence.

- Domestic violence is more common than most people realize. It is usually not a one-time, isolated occurrence or a single physical attack, but is a pattern of coercion and control.

- About five percent of victims of domestic violence are men.

- If violence is an issue, ask yourself: "Do I feel safe in the relationship?" If the answer is "No" or "I'm not sure," it's time to look for professional help.

- As with domestic violence between adult couples, anger leading to violence between parents and their children — child abuse — occurs all too often.

- All forms of abuse, including physical abuse, affect a child's emotional development. A physical injury will most often heal, but the memory of abuse remains for a lifetime. Emotional abuse can involve frequent threats, yelling, humiliation, ignoring, and blaming.

- Nearly every community has laws to protect children from abuse, a child protective agency, an anonymous number to report abuse, a process to investigate reports of abuse, and supportive services to help families. Find the resources in your town.

- Child abuse is a lifetime issue, affecting future generations as well. If you're wondering whether to get outside help, err on the side of safety.

Specific Questions and Directions

1. What are common myths about domestic violence? (pp. 265–266)
2. What is the cycle of domestic violence? Why do women who are victims of domestic violence often avoid seeking help? Why do men who are victims often avoid seeking help? (pp. 267–268)
3. How does one decide whether or not she or he is a victim of domestic violence and should get help? (pp. 268–269)
4. How do the authors define child abuse? What constitutes emotional abuse? Physical abuse? (pp. 271–272)

5. How do people get help if child abuse touches their lives? What are common myths about reporting child abuse? (pp. 272–273)

6. What is meant by "err on the side of safety"? (p. 273)

ACTION STEPS

Apply the concepts in chapter 16 that relate to your situation involving family violence. If there is violence in your family, seek help now!

◆ ◆ ◆

CHAPTER 17: "AFTER THE FAMILY STORM — AND BEYOND" (PP. 276–285)

(NOTE: No Major Points in this final chapter.)

SPECIFIC QUESTIONS AND DIRECTIONS

1. What is meant by "the power of apology"? Why have apologies "gone out of style" in recent years? (pp. 277–278)

2. What is the price of resentment? (p. 279)

3. How could forgiveness help you? (pp. 279–282)

4. Discuss the sidebar on page 279, "I'm Sorry' Is Not Always an Apology."

5. How could self-forgiveness help you? (pp. 282-283)

ACTION STEPS

Apply the concepts in chapter 17 involving apologies and forgiveness. Continue to apply the other ideas you've learned from reading the book and class discussion.

References

Dinkmeyer, Don, Sr., McKay, Gary D. and Dinkmeyer, Don, Jr. (1997) *STEP Session Guide* (in the *Leader's Resource Guide* for *Systematic Training for Effective Parenting*). Circle Pines, MN: American Guidance Service.

Dinkmeyer, Don, Sr., McKay, Gary D. and Dinkmeyer, Don, Jr. (1980) *Leader's Manual* (for *Systematic Training for Effective Teaching*). Bowling Green, KY: CMTI-Press, and Tucson, AZ: CMTI-West.

McKay, Gary D. and Maybell, Steven A. (2004) *Calming the Family Storm: Anger Management for Moms, Dads and All the Kids.* Atascadero, CA: Impact Publishers.

Soltz, Vicki. (1967) *Study Group Leader's Manual* (to be used with *Children the Challenge* by Dreikurs and Soltz). Chicago: Alfred Adler Institute.

Books with _Impact_

Calming the Family Storm
Anger Management for Moms, Dads, and All the Kids
Gary D. McKay, Ph.D. and Steven A. Maybell, Ph.D.
Softcover: $16.95   320 pages
Calming the Family Storm is a practical manual of helpful aids for handling the inevitable anger that every family experiences. Helps families work on the changes that will result in less anger, more effective expression of the anger you do experience, and a happier and more harmonious family life.

Anger Management
The Complete Treatment Guidebook for Practitioners
Howard Kassinove, Ph.D. and R. Chip Tafrate, Ph.D.
Softcover: $27.95   320 pages
The field of anger management is cluttered with fiction, myth, and wishful thinking. Here is a research-based and empirically validated "anger episode model," presented in a desktop manual for practitioners. Kassinove and Tafrate are themselves distinguished practitioners, researchers, and teachers in the field of anger management and their book offers a comprehensive state-of-the-art program that can be implemented almost immediately in any practice setting.

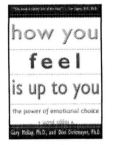

How You Feel Is Up To You
The Power of Emotional Choice (2nd Edition)
Gary D. McKay, Ph.D. and Don Dinkmeyer, Sr., Ph.D.
Softcover: $14.95   272 pages
Put "the power of emotional choice" to work for you. Learn to take responsibility for your emotions, enhance your awareness of feelings, and manage anger, anxiety, depression, guilt and stress. You can turn your feelings from liabilities ("I'm a victim.") into assets ("I can manage!). You can decide how you want to feel!

Parenting After Divorce
A Guide to Resolving Conflicts and Meeting Your Children's Needs
Philip M. Stahl, Ph.D.
Softcover: $15.95   192 pages
Here at last is a realistic perspective on divorce and its effects on children. Featuring knowledgeable advice from an expert custody evaluator, packed with real-world examples, this book avoids idealistic assumptions, and offers practical help for divorcing parents, custody evaluators, family court counselors, marriage and family therapists, and others interested in the well-being of children.

Time for a Better Marriage
Training in Marriage Enrichment
Jon Carlson, Psy.D. and Don Dinkmeyer, Sr., Ph.D.
Softcover: $15.95   144 pages   81/2" x 11"
A systematic, practical model for building marriage skills, providing tools to help make marriages more rewarding, effective, and satisfying by showing couples how to encourage each other, resolve conflict, communicate effectively, maintain equality in the relationship, and make better choices. Includes communication exercises, "marriage meetings," self-evaluation questionnaires, planning charts, review questions, many extra features.

**Please see following page for more
Books with Impact**

More Books with *Impact*

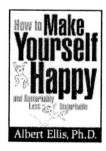